Motherhood is a paramount journey.
It is best to travel light.

The Uncluttered Mother

Free Up Your Space, Mind & Heart

DANA LAQUIDARA

DeVorss Publications
Camarillo, California

For my three daughters, my inspiration.

There are two ways
to do motherhood.

The first way is in a state of being overwhelmed in which you are overburdened and overstuffed. This way leaves a woman desperate for relief but in the habit of gathering more—more of some elusive thing that will bring you relief.

The second way brings happiness, joy, and a deep and satisfying peace.

This book is about the second way.

The Uncluttered Mother

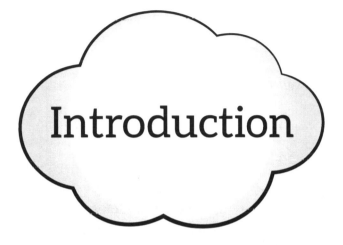

Introduction

Simplicity is the ultimate sophistication.

—Leonardo da Vinci

If ever there was a time in your life to simplify, this is it! You are on a wonderful, sacred journey that could potentially bury you alive in clutter, activities, chores, and so much else. *So much else.*

It is unlikely that anything else you ever do will have the same potential to both overwhelm you and fill you with joy as motherhood. It is this dichotomy that led me to be ruthless in finding out what would bring about more of the latter. More joy, more peace, more creativity.

As a mom with three grown children and plenty of hindsight, I wrote this book as a guide to keeping motherhood light. I hope my words inspire and empower you to take charge of motherhood, in turn making you feel lighter, freer, and more in touch with the truth of who you are. Excavating your authentic self will make you a happier woman and a better mother. It is as simple—and as challenging—as that.

As I finish writing this book, we are in the throes of a worldwide pandemic brought on by COVID-19 (the coronavirus). People are fearful for their health, their jobs, their loved ones. The situation is both enormous and largely out of our control. It is a reminder that life is fragile, and all we can do, all too often, is our best.

Introduction

Every choice we make either adds to the chaos of life or soothes us and those around us in some way. Our day-to-day decisions either add or subtract from our physical, mental, and spiritual health, whether in the midst of a crisis or on a typical, nondescript day. *Our choices* are all we can control, in everything. It is no accident, at this time, that you are being called to mindfulness and wholeness. We are all interconnected, and life is requiring a raising of the collective consciousness. Mothers, along with everyone else, must rise to the occasion. The ripple effects of our choices are astounding.

How you "do motherhood" will greatly affect not only your own happiness, but that of your children, your partner, and to some extent, your community. Being an uncluttered mother won't prevent all the challenges you'll face, but it will free you up to respond to those challenges mindfully and intelligently, adding light to your family and to the world beyond.

Clutter & Calendars

Things which matter most must never be at the mercy of things which matter least.

—Johann Wolfgang Von Goethe

The Sweet Space of Less

I detest clutter. It feels bad to me, almost like suffocating, whereas leaning into minimalism feels like freedom and clarity. It takes conscious effort to maintain clarity of space and mind and is a quest I feel is worthy of writing an entire book about. I particularly notice that simplifying my environment improves my writing, as if the space in my home invites the muse to settle in and move my pen across the page without distraction. My mind is open to inspiration, the words sweeping through me uninhibited and unencumbered. Tangible or intangible, it's all the same to me. Space clutter equals mind clutter. One leads to the other and they become one fog that traps precious energy, stalling progress and making forward motion a slow walk through quicksand.

I get strangely excited for anyone who tells me they're cleaning out their garage or a closet. I know what it will do to their mind and spirit. The clearing-out will invite the flow of something good, something nourishing that finds an opening and trickles in. Call it an obsession or a passion, but I'm letting it manifest itself from me to you and take form in this book. I hope it inspires you to take a step or two toward simplifying your own life and maintaining a simplicity I know you'll love.

Clutter

I want you to take charge of your home and your life. I want you to get your groove back, one simplifying tactic at a time. But it'll go better if you're all in.

Are you in?

Let's start at home. Literally, in your home. I haven't seen it, but I bet there's too much stuff. Where does it all come from? If you're buying it, take pause. If too many items come into your home in the way of gifts, call a moratorium on material gifts. Kindly, graciously, but with conviction. Make sure people understand you don't want stuff. You'd be surprised how many friends and relatives will appreciate not having to figure out what to get you.

But how do you get rid of the stuff already cluttering up your life?

Make a game of going through stuff with your kids. I used to play this with mine. "Let's see who can find ten things we can give away." Let your kids partake in going through clothes. What fits now? What should be passed down to a sibling or cousin or donated to charity? But don't limit yourself to clothes. Add in games they've outgrown, toys they don't play with, and knick-knacks you don't remember getting. Make piles. Have a fashion show. Have fun. We're often looking for things to do with our children. This can provide hours, if not days, of at-home projects with your kids.

If there is no joy to be had for you in this, then do not involve your children just yet. The idea is to show them that organizing and simplifying can be fun. If you do this in the heavy spirit of *Mom is overwhelmed and needs you to go through your stuff right this minute, dammit,* well, you know how that will end. Tears. Anxiety. Stubbornness. Sheer futility. But if you are excited to simplify, then your joy will be contagious. It's all in the attitude.

And remember, it is easier not to bring too many toys into the house than it is to take them away. It's also an option to cycle the toys through, putting some away and then swapping them out periodically. Children are overwhelmed by too many things. It can cause apprehension, distraction, and crankiness, not to mention a mess. A giant mess. So, rather than give them the gift of toys, give them the gift of open spaces, the great outdoors, and your attention. One game played with a loving parent is worth more than a hundred games on a shelf.

•

What about your own closet? Your bedroom? The kitchen, the gadgets, the papers, the magazines? Go through all of it. Maybe you do it all at once, or maybe you set aside an hour each Sunday until you are satisfied. Whichever way you choose, don't skip this part of simplifying. Clearing out clutter will raise your energy levels like you won't believe. It feels amazing, like creating an opening scene in a play from which the rest of the action flows. It is a simple action, yet a powerful reminder that you are a creative, free-spirited being and can make changes that feel tremendous.

What will you go through first? How will you become more mindful of all the things in your life?

Here are a few ideas to get you started. See where the momentum takes you:

Bedroom
This should be a sacred space of rejuvenation and intimacy, so carefully pick and choose what you allow in this room. Clothes strewn about, a television in the room, and dust on the furniture all detract significantly from the atmosphere. Warm colors, soy candles, clean sheets, and an organized closet can transform a bedroom into

a place you truly feel welcome, whether alone or with a partner. It will *feel* different; better. Don't give it less attention than you'd give any other room. In fact, give it *more*.

How can you open up the space in this room? Are you hanging on to clothing that no longer fits your lifestyle, your tastes, or your body? Before you bring in something different and better, get rid of the old. What about your sleepwear, your footwear, your jewelry? Discernment is empowering.

Now, what about your child's bedroom? Can you encourage him or her to take pride in keeping it organized and tidy, as well as technology-free? Kids not getting enough sleep due to screen time well past a reasonable bedtime has become a real problem. They depend on parents to set the ground rules. Some families have a basket that all members put their cell phones or other electronic devices in before going to bed. It's a healthy habit best implemented from the beginning.

Bathroom

This room should be clean with hints of vitality: plants, a splash of color, simplicity. Reconsider those fuzzy toilet covers that are one more thing to launder, as well as any overflow of toiletries. Get rid of unnecessary makeup items—decide what works best on you and toss the rest. It's a relief to simplify the options. For example, Clinique Black Honey lipstick looks good on everyone, but if you want a less expensive option, the Revlon equivalent is Fig Jam. Maybe there is one color of eye shadow that looks best on you; so why hold on to the others?

For your children, you will be setting an example by creating an uncomplicated, uncluttered beauty routine. Daughters, especially, are watching you. Believe me, I know the pressure of this. Having raised three daughters of my own, I had three sets of eyes constantly watching me, learning what it means to move through this world as a female. And although a beauty regime is surely not at the top of this list of "things that are important," it doesn't mean it's not on the list at all. Being confident and efficient about your routine matters, as does modeling the philosophy that no beauty product in the world is a substitute for what you put *inside* your body. If you're buying products to cover up for a poor diet and not enough water, change your priorities until you find you can get rid of that beauty product, too.

Kitchen

In a world where we generally eat three meals a day (not to mention the occasional snack), which room is more important than this one? This is where we keep the food that either fuels or depletes our energy and our bodies. It is also where we commune with family and friends, hopefully in an atmosphere of healthy abundance. It is where children first witness, and then help, prepare meals. Not only is this a fabulous way to spend time together, it is a useful skill that will help sustain them throughout life and be appreciated by future partners and their children.

Nothing reminds me of stuck gunk in a body more than a dirty fridge. It is truly a pet peeve of mine, and therefore I give the fridge at least a cursory wipe down before any big trip to the grocery store. Life-giving food deserves to be sheltered in a clean refrigerator, free of spilled liquids, expired items, and forgotten leftovers. An organized pantry is a clean fridge's fraternal twin. Seeing at a glance what we have stored or can easily access makes food preparation a joy. Is the energy of your kitchen murky, gunky, and askew, or is it clean, clear, and healthful?

Living Area

It can be difficult to get every person in the family to agree on the standards of neatness in this shared space. You may want to tidy things up to get rid of the excess, but your spouse or kids won't "play along." So, here's my advice: *Be the change you want to see*. Organize and tidy what you can, and make it obvious where things go. Even toddlers will pick up their things if there are designated places for them—coat hooks they can reach, baskets or shelves for toys, a bench or closet for shoes. Keep your own items put away, as well as any shared items. Once surfaces are relatively clear, people are less inclined to dump items on them. It is true that messy surroundings bother some more than others, but you must be the one to set the standard when no one else will. And then kindly, strategically encourage others to follow suit.

Car

Your car symbolizes where you are going in life. Are you moving forward and navigating from one stage to another or going nowhere sitting in a mess you've made? Clean out any clutter in your car to invite clarity and overcome stagnation. You are in the driver's seat—make it a good ride. If you have teens or young adults who drive, teach them that responsible car ownership includes keeping the car clean. Operating this massive piece of machinery requires maintenance, skill, and most importantly, undistracted driving. I know that keeping a car tidy seems fairly insignificant, but it sets the tone for being on the road. You can even make it a stipulation for being allowed to drive the car at all. If we agree that clearing clutter clears the mind, can we agree that it is especially important while driving?

Décor, Simply Put

My desire to minimize the amount of stuff I own includes all manner of decorations. I was never one for knickknacks, seeing them as moderately cute dust collectors that our children will someday have to feel guilty about throwing away. My preference to keep my indoor space simple and uncluttered doesn't change when holidays come around. In fact, I've found it all sorts of fun to simplify my decorating year-round. I have been delighted by how easy and affordable it is to change the seasonal look with subtle but aesthetically pleasing décor.

Now, my decorating strategy may be too sparse for some. I freely admit that it really is a matter of personal preference. And like clearing out a closet or a cabinet, I can't quite put my finger on why such simplicity feels so good to me. I look at the subtle sparkle of a simple décor, and it feels like the spirit of each season has room to breathe.

Clear glass vases that hold dried flowers during spring and summer can be filled with vibrant red silk flowers in winter. Table runners are easy pieces to change with the season. Clear lights can be draped over large plants to brighten up a dreary November. Vines of holly in winter, or artificial foliage in fall, can line a mantel perfectly.

Happily, I don't own holiday dishes. That requires extra storage space, time to take them out and wash them, time to put them away, and effort to search for new pieces to replace the ones that break. My dishes are neutral, which allows the napkins, table runner, and holiday food to announce the festivities. My boxes of decorations are minimal, making my trips to the attic few and far between. It brings me joy to beautify and shift my environment with ease.

Seeing Christmas lights and wreaths up well into March makes me wish the owners would give themselves permission to bring the decorating down a notch to a manageable level both at the start of the season and at the end. *What goes up, really should come down.* Or consider skipping the holiday decorating altogether. Any visual pleasure that takes place over the holidays surely is offset by the unsightliness of Christmas décor when spring approaches! Like nail polish that stays on for far too long, chipped and unlovely, some things are better left undone from the beginning.

What's on Your Calendar?

We live in a child-centric society, but the way I see it, it's good for kids (and moms, too) to step away from the kid-friendly entertainment and bring children into the adult world. Kids know when you are spending time with them just to appease them and when you truly want their company. Seek them out occasionally to play a game or to accomplish a task together, even if it does take you twice as long. It fills a child's heart to know you want to spend time with them, not just shuffling them to activities or depositing them into a kids' zone of sorts, but actually spending device-free time with them, complete with conversation and your undivided attention.

When we have cleaned up our own restlessness and resist the pull of needless distractions, we become content with the simplicity of this.

Does your family's calendar overwhelm you? Do you believe your children partaking in more activities than you can comfortably, happily accommodate is acceptable?

What children need most are happy parents. They do not *have* to attend every birthday party they are invited to or play every sport or join every club. They need family time. They need to see parents engaging in their own interests once in a while. They need time to be alone to dream and think and play and discover what they truly like, without too much outside influence telling them what they *should* like.

Perhaps you are afraid they'll miss out if they cut back on activities. Afterall, *everyone else* is doing so much!

What if everyone else is suffering too?

What if you became the person who didn't complain about the over-busyness but instead changed something? What if your answer to "How are you?" was no longer "Crazy busy," but "Great! I'm rested. I'm reading this great book. ..."

What if you spoke to your children like this:

Our current family calendar has gotten much too hectic. It's not healthy for us to continue at this pace. I would like your help in figuring out the things that aren't so very loved that can be eliminated. If it's difficult for you to choose, I will help you. You can each keep one activity per season (or whatever you deem reasonable).

The amount of enjoyment or fulfillment an activity provides should outweigh the resources that it consumes. When an activity exhausts us or keeps us from having the quiet moments that nourish our spirits, we suffer. Our children suffer. It is often in the quiet moments— the unstructured time, those extra minutes we linger over while saying goodnight—that a child will speak what's in her heart. It is during times of boredom that a person's creativity will emerge, surprising us with ideas, insights, and a rich connection to our inner lives. This time is precious, but we have to leave room for it.

For every activity scheduled, ask yourself: *Why are we doing this? What do we stand to gain, and what do we stand to lose?* Then choose wisely, according to yours and your family's unique needs.

School

This is the toughest area of all for some. I've been there. When my children were very young, they did not love school. They did not like the noisy bus and the crowded cafeteria and the homework that cut into their free time and creativity. They did not like spending six or seven hours a day with a hoard of kids and teachers directing their every move. And who can blame them? There are some necessary, efficient, and productive elements to mass education, but let's face it, a one-size-fits-all anything is going to have its problems.

But maybe your kids love school, or at least tolerate it pretty well, which is fantastic! This part will be easier for you. Perhaps any school-related overwhelming comes from the various duties you find yourself with—signing permission slips, supervising homework, attending teacher conferences, and staying involved.

Whether your kids love school or not, some school stress is unavoidable if your kids, well... *attend school*. School is a 180-day per year commitment, with homework.

It is worth mentioning that the temperament of your child can make a significant difference in how much energy he has left after his school day. An extroverted child gains energy from being around lots of people, whereas an introverted child's energy is drained. Only you and your child can determine how much energy school is extracting from your precious children. Once you figure that out, you can acknowledge it and plan accordingly.

Simplify what you can (home environment, extracurriculars, etc.) so that what you have less control over (the school day and the homework) won't put you over the edge. If you've simplified your family's schedule, routines, and environment, there will undoubtedly be more family time, and more time to recharge between each school day. This goes a long way to keep anxiety at bay, for you and your kids.

Let's not pretend that school isn't a full-time job for your kids (and in some cases, particularly if your child has special needs, a part-time one for you). It just is. So, give it the room it requires and don't fill in every free hour around it.

•

I cannot leave it unsaid that after centuries of little change, the entity that we know as "school" may be shifting. Our world is changing, and many aspects of education are being reevaluated, largely out of necessity. I think that we are being invited to look at the big picture, the whole child, and reconsider our obsession with testing, compliance, and trying to ensure that every child knows every fact. What kind of education will allow our children to dream big, to engage in worthy projects of their own choosing, and to become lifelong learners? Will it be online, more global, more intrinsically driven? Will it be child-led learning, home schooling, or merely a change in the way public schools are run? The answer will not be the same for everyone, and may indeed be some combination of these and more, but the wheels are in motion for change. If we loosen our grip on what we have known education to be, we can welcome the possibility of something more authentic and nourishing to the young hearts and minds of our children and many generations to follow.

Chores

It is normal and healthy to prioritize our children and their well-being and interests. But raising our children with the belief that the family completely revolves around them and their over-packed schedules while the mundane chores of life magically get done (probably while their parents should be sleeping or relaxing), or they don't get done at all (because who has any time left?) does not serve them well.

There are chores in life. Lots of chores. Food needs to be purchased and prepared. Cars need to be maintained and toilets need to be scrubbed and bills need to be paid and finances need to be organized and pets need to go to the vet and laundry needs be done and dishwashers need to be emptied. Rugs get vacuumed and trash gets put out. Appointments get scheduled and drains get unclogged and papers get filed and mail gets opened and birthday gifts get ordered and thank-you notes get written.

Along the way, some of us forgot to factor in all the time it takes to get things done that are required to live a decently organized and grown-up life. Or we forgot to let the kids bear witness to that, let alone have them take part in it.

There is work to do—often tedious, boring work—that must get done within the waking hours that we have in a day.

Young children can help Mom or Dad prepare dinner, water plants, sort laundry, or whatever other task or activity you care to invite them to partake in.

As far as I can tell, it's not only okay but pertinent to involve each family member in some of these tasks. They are part of life. You are raising children who you hope will one day function as responsible adults. Buffering them from the tedium of life is unfair to you and them.

You don't have to be the martyr who stays up late to do the chores no one else notices. You also don't have to live in a state of disorganization. Every family has their own needs and circumstances, but no one over the age of four should be oblivious to the nuts and bolts of running a home. Someday your children will need to do these chores for themselves, and they will be so much better off if they've been included in the stuff of life all along.

Volunteering

Let's face it—when the school, church, or other institution falls short of its budget, resources, or manpower, it's usually women who step in and fill the need. Giving to others joyously makes us happy. But giving so much of our time and energy means we have nothing left for ourselves, which can make us resentful. Being a mother requires a lot of giving, as you know. Hence the term *caregiving.* I suggest you tailor the amount of volunteering you do to respect your own limits. Your time is valuable, and so is your life-force energy. Use it wisely and save some just for you.

Another point I want to make is that even though we often volunteer on behalf of our children, we mustn't forget that what our children need the most from us is our presence. Many years ago, I read an essay that I can no longer find called "Chasing Mother." In it, the author described a childhood in which her mother was her Girl Scout leader, her Little

League coach, a school volunteer, and so many other things. She knew this was all to benefit her, the child. But what she wanted more than anything was her mother's attention, one on one. She felt she was always chasing this attention, trying to capture one iota of her tired, busy mom's time, just for the two of them.

Volunteering is a noble endeavor, but for Women Who Give Too Much, it can be a trap. Figure out if you've crossed the line between giving with love and running your own well dry. Better to give a little and get a lot back than to give everything and run out of time for what's most important.

Slack

Beware the Quantity Trap. Whether we are talking about the amount of stuff you own, the number of children you choose to have, or how cluttered you keep your calendar, the bottom line is this:

It is not about how much you *can* do; it's about how much is *best* to do. So, the next time you feel your head safely above water because you have caught up on tasks, on sleep, or whatever, resist the urge to take on more. Instead, relish the tranquility—the easy rhythm of your day; the sanity of the moment. When and if it is time to take on more, you will know. Love yourself enough to wait it out.

Having some slack is good for your quality of life and peace of mind. If you are already overwhelmed by the intensity of your life, unexpected events will leave you with no reserves to take on the added stressor. You may not have the energy, the time, the money, or anything else to face the latest crisis.

On October 31, 2018, my husband received a totally unexpected diagnosis. I will always remember the day that he received a call from the doctor who had his biopsy results. The small lump at his jawline was not uncommon. The doctor had been optimistic—cavalier even—but it turned out that his was not benign at all. It was a rare cancer of the parotid gland.

That evening, as it was getting dark, the time that little ones would start showing up at our door looking for treats, we realized we'd forgotten all about Halloween. We had no candy and were in no mood for visitors. We turned out most of the lights and sat in the near-dark living room, allowing this new reality to sit with us. We kept the trick-or-treaters at bay, but we were not alone. There was a wolf at the door, and it was Cancer.

Today my husband is doing well, but as I am sure you can imagine, this was an all-encompassing time as we planned for and he underwent daily radiation and weekly chemotherapy treatments. We kept multiple appointments and took on everything else a serious illness throws in one's court. It was traumatic, but not chaotic.

We were very fortunate to have good health insurance and supportive family nearby, as well as children who are well into adulthood; none of that can be discounted. But I also attribute the lack of utter turmoil to the simplicity of our lifestyle and the clarity with which we made decisions. We had room, not just in our lives, but in our psyches, to absorb the shock.

Many people have fewer options under such dire circumstances and much that is not in their control. But this book is about finding what you *can* change and making conscious choices so that you come closer and closer to living the life your soul intended. And I truly believe your soul intended you to have some slack, some breathing room.

The wolf comes knocking on every door, sooner or later. Whether it is illness, injury, death of a parent, job loss, divorce, or crisis with a child, we need grace to help carry us through. Leave room for grace.

The Tradition Wizard

I feel there is an entity that has too much control over people's celebrations: the Tradition Wizard. This wizard seems to wave his invisible wand and lull society into some sort of traditional trance. I know when I've fallen victim to him because I feel a dissonance between what I do and what I *want* to do. Who is this guy, anyway?

Traditions are usually founded on some practical purpose but often do not evolve with changing times and new information. Even so, the pressure to continue them is both strong and overt. So deep runs the pressure to abide by most public holiday traditions that commercialization is having a party nearly all year long. One holiday blends into another, stores run sales for several holidays simultaneously, some people plan their Halloween activities months in advance, and the Christmas season lasts longer than an actual season.

How can we live a clutter-free life if we are afraid to let go of what does not suit us?

I am not saying that traditions don't have their place. I realize there are many traditions, including some religious ones, which are important to a large portion of humanity. For the most part, I enjoy the big holidays, and I have loved creating some smaller traditions for my own family—traditions that revolve around reading and mealtimes and birthday celebrations. Self-created, they became habits that have made life sweeter.

But the Tradition Wizard is fierce and persistent. He comes around every year and hundreds of times in the course of a lifetime. Halloween, Valentine's Day, playing Santa, bar mitzvahs, birthdays, wedding showers, and on and on. Some of these traditions feel distracting, stressful, or forced, yet we feel like rebels if we don't partake.

Many people hold on to traditions like they do ingrained beliefs. To hear of anything different feels threatening. Outrageous even. They are the fierce supporters of the Tradition Wizard. They will not quit until he does. And he never does.

I don't care which traditions my now-grown children choose to follow. I only care that they choose them consciously and respect that other people get to choose for themselves. Deviating from the norm can cause stress and therefore takes courage. I hope they always hold firm to what they believe is right for them and not what they think is *expected* of them.

When my oldest daughter got married, the advice I gave her was that there are no rules regarding your wedding. She could pick and choose which traditions to include or leave out. She considered whether throwing the bouquet—a tradition that dates back to the Middle Ages— was appropriate for her celebration. We all know the drill. The single girls line up to compete in catching the bouquet, and the lucky one who does is said to be the next who will marry. This implies that all the single girls want to be married, and as soon as possible. Is that right in this day and age? We could, in fact, question all of the wedding traditions, from the father giving the bride away to the ancient tradition of the bride covering her face with a veil lest the groom in an arranged marriage change his mind when he sees her. You can choose to keep all of them or none of them. But you should at least *choose*.

Any tradition can be carried out simply out of preference, or as a matter of style, or fun, with no implications. All I am saying is that they should be chosen consciously. And to do that, you have to remember that it is a *choice*. There's always a choice.

Some traditions and rituals are pernicious or wrought with a history of oppression, while others serve a purpose for some but are meaningless to others. *All are optional.* The more pressure we feel about a tradition, the more we should question it.

I say look the Tradition Wizard in the eye and make up your own mind. It's the only way to take away his power.

Have a Mediocre Holiday

I hope I reach you before The Madness sweeps you away. Chances are it doesn't have you in its grip quite yet, though it could be close. I certainly bet you think you're succumbing.

And just what is The Madness? It is Everything You Must Do in Order to Have a Great Holiday. It is fulfilling grand expectations, whether your own or those of someone else's. Maybe your mother's or mother-in-law's, or your spouse's or your kids'? Does the mere thought of everything you have to do to ensure that everyone in your family has a great holiday grab you at the sternum and trickle down to your gut? Does it excite you...or does it hit you with a twinge of dread?

If your answer is dread, here is my suggestion: Change the goal from having a fabulous holiday to having a mediocre one. Mediocre holidays are much gentler on the psyche. You know the saying, *What goes up must come down*? The holiday mood—anticipation, excitement, *chaos*— not only has to come from somewhere, it has to go somewhere when it's over! The time, money, and energy it takes to create an *amazing* holiday is likely siphoned from your daily life. Before the festivities, you're working on adrenaline, anticipation, and possible guilt. Afterward, you crash.

Now, what if you decide not to steal from whatever makes your daily life good? Your exercise routine, time with loved ones, alone time, a creative endeavor—whatever it is that keeps you sane and happy—what if you guarded it with your life? Because *every ordinary day IS your life.*

During the holidays, I want to be with family, enjoy some good food, and open a few carefully chosen presents. But I also want to enjoy them before the holidays. And after. No rushing, no stress, no frenzy, no crash. There's something to be said for being a holiday underachiever. I'm saying no to the high of an amazing holiday season, and yes to the peace of a mediocre one. I invite you to join me if you like. Maybe this year you skip the holiday cards, or cut down on the baking. Put up fewer decorations, have others bring a favorite dish to the meal, and don't fuss over your children's holiday clothing.

Perhaps some people thrive on the frenzy of an amazing holiday, but for the rest of us, a mediocre holiday is a *happy* holiday.

Ordinary Days

Why do we change our daily routine around the holidays? If we've established what works best for us on our ordinary days, doesn't altering it for special days make us worse off? How about when we alter it day after day in preparation for the holiday?

Often the habits that support our own wellness are the first to go, as evidenced by emptier yoga classes and crowded malls that time of year. It's a funny phenomenon, really, that we take what many of us consider to be the most sacred time of year and plunge into self-neglect, often with bells on.

I enjoy the holidays so much more when I don't allow them to take over my life, and in particular, my *lifestyle*. Holidays are fun, but I love ordinary days. My dopamine levels are doing just great on ordinary days, thank you. I'm not really looking for that shot of WOW. I'd rather push my limits in a completely different area of life.

For better or worse, it doesn't take much "extra" to make me feel out of sorts. Multitasking is a lie meant to turn mothers into martyrs. A focused life is so much more satisfying than a scattered, ten-balls-in-the-air one. And although each holiday or family vacation *can* be fun, the planning of such events undoubtedly adds another ball to the juggling act of life. This is okay if we are doing just fine in our day-to-day-lives, but otherwise, we should funnel that energy into making our ordinary days great instead.

I don't want to give up writing or yoga or meditation or cooking healthy meals for days or weeks leading up to a holiday just to make myself happy for a few hours on a single day. I'll take all of the things that make me happy on ordinary days over the few things that make me happy on a given holiday every single time.

Around the time of my high-school prom, our history teacher asked the girls why we were making hair appointments for the big event. "I assume the way you wear your hair every day is the way you think it looks best, so why change it for prom?" he asked. I thought he had a good point, which I guess is why I still remember his statement so many years later. But taking his questions further, there is something relevant to life here, not just to proms and hairdos.

Women have been proclaiming loud and clear about the everyday mental and emotional clutter we carry, since it causes all sorts of stress and fatigue. Then, when the holidays come, we take on more. What if you decided that all the extra energy required for the holidays should not be siphoned from your creative well? What if you did just enough to bring you joy and no more?

Toning down the holidays is good for you, your family, *and* your creativity. And anything that fuels creativity fuels the human spirit.

Identifying your ideal level of holiday stimulation, and drawing the line there is no easy task. It has a lot to do with temperament, personal preference, and a dozen other things, including family pressure or expectations. But I think it's worth figuring out for ourselves when to shake things up (and when your ordinary hairdo will do!).

Suggested Reading

The Curated Closet
by Anuschka Rees (2016, Ten Speed Press)

How to Be a Happier Parent
by KJ Dell'Antonia (2020, Avery)

The Joy of Less
by Francine Jay (2016, Chronicle)

The Life-Changing Magic of Tidying Up
by Marie Kondo (2014, Ten Speed Press)

168 Hours: You Have More Time Than You Think by Laura Vanderkam (2010, Portfolio)

Health
& Habits

Motivation is what gets you started.
Habit is what keeps you going.

—Jim Rohn

Dear Overwhelmed Mothers

These days, we hear a lot about the mental workload of moms. Moms are tired and stressed because of the often-exhausting life they've created for themselves and their families. There is so much to keep track of, so much to think about and plan for and be attentive to, and it's all falling on the shoulders—and or brains—of moms.

It's the cross we bear in these modern times, right? The weight of the family is on our backs, as is the cost of keeping our kids engaged, involved, and happy. "Men just don't get it," mothers are saying. Dads are doing a lot too, and we don't deny that, but they *just don't know the half of it*. Compared to moms, say so many moms, *dads are slumbering*.

Is it that men are refusing to share the full responsibility of parenting? Or that women pay much more attention to the details and minutia of raising children and maintaining households?

Do women simply put more pressure on themselves to do it all perfectly because they feel their homes and children are a reflection of themselves? Or maybe we take on more than is necessary "for the good of our children," even as the added burdens crush us. Which stressors for moms are indicative of dads not doing their fair share, and which ones are a sign of moms choosing to do too much? And for single moms, can you share the burden with other single parents? Fewer people live near extended family than ever before, and if you're also the only adult in your household, you may need to get more creative in your resourcefulness.

Moms read and discuss articles about the unique burdens of motherhood, particularly working mothers, while nodding their heads in agreement, with the words resonating and feeling just a bit better knowing they are not alone. It is validating to hear someone accurately name the stress you feel and realize that so many others relate right along with you.

And that's important. It's important to be heard and understood. But it's more important to take action and solve those problems.

This book is meant to help you do that. It's meant to be a nudge forward. So, it's time to move on from Feeling Understood to Doing Something About It. You are the goddess of your family and more powerful than you are giving yourself credit for. Imagine taking charge of yourself, your family life, your stress levels, and your Mental Workload, as we've been calling it.

None of this is easy, I know. And trust me, I empathize. But as women, I think we've gone as far as we can go with the camaraderie and the complaining. It is time to take action. It is time to change the things we can change.

•

Once upon a time not so long ago, with three kids in elementary school and holidays bearing down on me, I felt overwhelmed. A little bit angry. A lot disappointed.

My kids' childhoods were flying by in a succession of reminders, commands, and have-tos:

Time for school,
time for homework,
brush your teeth,
time for bed.
Do this, don't forget that.
The laundry.
The tickets.
The birthday card.
Did I sign those forms?
The dog is due for a grooming.

It felt nearly impossible to stay in the moment. Their lives were on fast-forward while I was in slow motion. And then I said, "ENOUGH!" There is something in me that is not very tolerant of unhappiness and not at all comforted by numbers. For that, I am grateful. I became deeply motivated by the desire for simplicity.

Let me be clear, ladies. I know your mental energy is being taxed, and you are juggling a lot. But like I said, you are the Goddess of your home. Well, if you have to be the Executive too, then you best be the one to spark a change in the family dynamics. Instead of you single-handedly making the rules, help others realize what it takes and the burden it places on you. By including your family in the changes and inviting them to be part of the solution, they become invested in the results. If something is not working for everyone in the family—and that means Mama too—then it isn't working!

There's a lot of inertia going on, and perhaps you've found yourself floating down the Current of Being Overwhelmed. This life counts. Don't just try to manage your time. Manage yourself, your habits, your energy. You are encouraged to make changes so that eighteen years—potentially a quarter of your life—does not go by in a fog of stress.

My top three priorities are family, health, and writing. What are yours? Name your top three. Four, at most. I don't believe we have room in our lives for more than that without everything becoming diluted and meaningless. Now, with every choice you make, ask yourself, *Does this fall under one of my top priorities?* If not, say no to it. Choose your yeses carefully according to that one question. Reassess everything you do. Fewer things pulling at you allows you to be present in your own life. When everything but your top priorities falls away, you will have found your core self, and that is a beautiful thing. *You* are beautiful.

Find solid ground. Breathe. *Simplify.*

The Life-Changing Magic of Meditation

There is so much information available supporting the benefits of meditation, and I invite you to read much of that scientific evidence when you get the chance. For now, I am simply going to say that meditation enables us to keep our promises to ourselves, make good and healthy choices, and access a wealth of wisdom and information not immediately accessible by our buzzing minds.

You only have to allot ten minutes a day to meditation to reap some significant benefits, including better sleep, stress reduction, clarity, and peace. Who doesn't have ten minutes? I can almost guarantee you that once it becomes a habit, you will look forward to it and want to extend the time for it.

I recommend approaching it like an experiment. If you don't currently meditate, then you know what a typical day *without* meditation is like. Why not see what your day is like *with* meditation? How about a week with meditation? The results may astound you.

Writer Natalie Goldberg describes our unconscious, or what she calls our "Wild Mind," as a big sky. It holds all our dreams and all our answers. We all have access to this All That Is, but not everyone dips into it as often they should—and those unable to tune out the noise of the world may miss it altogether.

Natalie tells us to picture a little dot in the center of the sky. That, she says, is what Zen calls "Monkey Mind," or what Western psychology calls part of the conscious mind. Goldberg says we give almost all of our attention to that little dot, which says, "You can't do that; shouldn't even try; do this instead."

So, while Wild Mind surrounds us like a big sky, powerful and vast, and waits for us, whispering the truth to us, we get swept away from it for days, years, even a lifetime, because we are focusing only on the Monkey Mind. We focus on the dot instead of what's beyond it.

That we have access to it, though, is our greatest gift. If you want to experience the magic that meditation will bring to your life but are turned off to the idea of sitting in silence, you can try one of several fantastic meditation apps such as Headspace or Calm to guide you through a session.

Meditation will reorganize your brain and lead you toward better choices, moment by moment. It is the guiding force that has you putting one steady foot in front of the other until you realize you have ended up in a better place.

If you take only one thing away from this book, I hope it is the desire to start meditating. I can tell you what I know about living an uncluttered life, but living it and experiencing the uncluttered life is up to you. And the greatest wisdom *for you* will come from your *own* intuition. Meditation is a proven way to access that.

Beyond Mind Clutter

To some extent, we are all addicted to thinking. It's such an acceptable affliction and everyone is doing it. There is no known support group or treatment plan for this. No one's likely to come at us with an intervention for excessive thinking. We are free to think our lives away!

Yet, overthinking can cause anxiety, stress, and judgment.

Thoughts are magnetic and can act like thieves, pulling our consciousness away to take us further and further out of the present moment.

And when we exit the present moment, we miss out on a lot.

Besides reducing stress and anxiety, staying present can solve an ordinary problem or spark a novel idea in *any* area of life, even the most mundane. Present-moment living allows us access to ideas, answers, and inspirations that *just aren't available to our rigid, overthinking brains.*

Peace, clarity, and creativity become available when we toss our mind clutter and grow still. After struggling with something, completely disengaging from the problem often gives us a better chance of solving it.

In other words, when our conscious mind shuts the heck up, we can finally hear the faintest whisper of an idea from the subconscious mind. In our most uncluttered, authentic state, we have access to brilliance.

The subconscious mind has so much more to draw on than our chattering, conscious mind. So, how do we access it? How do we access mindfulness?

How indeed?

Young children are naturally mindful all the time. They live in the moment, at least until the grown-ups pull them out. We hook their attention with questions about yesterday or requests to "get ready" for the next thing.

For most of us, as we get older, it takes more concerted effort to be mindful. Often, it's when we're engaged in a favorite pastime that we become mindful. If there is an activity you love doing, I hope you can do it often. Meditation, yoga, journaling, jogging, walking, dancing, and other forms of exercise (anything that gets you out of your head and into your *body*) can induce mindfulness. So can knitting, gardening, or any repetitive task that engages the mind *just barely*. A window opens to the subconscious, letting in bright ideas like bright sunlight. At the very least, there is peace. We are matching the energy of a higher consciousness, and that is a beautiful thing.

Ideally, we'd be so good at being mindful that we wouldn't need anything to *get us there*. I'm not there yet, so I depend on certain things like yoga and meditation to pull me back into the present. What are some pleasant or fun things you can do that will place you firmly in the present moment? And what will it feel like to let go of the struggle and welcome all the brilliance that is yours when you do?

Any form of self-care will lead to mindfulness. In fact, the more self-care, the better.

Clearing a Path for the Good Stuff

Decluttering your environment helps clear your head. Simplifying your life can lead to fewer distractions pulling you out of the present moment by managing the little things.

If you take care of the small things,
the big things take care of themselves.
You can gain more control over your life
by paying closer attention to the little things.

—Emily Dickinson

After I discovered this poignant quote by Emily Dickinson, I sat back and thought about what she might consider to be the "small things" in her lifetime, and if they're still relevant today. Here are a few little things that can clear the path to the good big things.

What are the little things?

Drinking water
Getting enough sleep
Decluttering
Keeping only what you love
Breathing deeply
Exercising
Hugging a child
Replacing a button
Hanging a picture
Thinking good thoughts
Doing paperwork
Eating vegetables
Saying kind words
Donating stuff

What are the big things?

Harmony

Inspiration

Clarity

Insight

Healing

Hope

Decision making

Peace

Fulfillment

Joy

Freedom

Success

Love

Creativity

Truth

Ideas

Courage

How does taking care of little things lead to big things?

Everything in this entire universe is made up of energy. From solid things like food to ethereal things like thoughts, you name it. This is not a new phenomenon. This is also not a New Age theory or an unscientific guess. This has been true for all of eternity.

Einstein reported that "...both the physical plane of our reality of matter and the abstract reality of our mind are made up of energy patterns." Every cell, thing, thought, word, and morsel of food has a vibrational frequency.

There is positive energy, negative energy, and neutral energy. All of them are easy to decipher. How do you feel after doing something? Saying something? Thinking something? Being in a particular environment? What adds to your energy, and what takes away from it? Find those things that increase your energy and do them as often as possible.

In case you hadn't noticed, children pick up on our energy like wool picks up lint. If your energy is clean, your child will bask in it. It will be calming, comforting, and inspiring to them. If it is murky and low, he will become the neediest child on the block, guaranteed.

The truth is, we determine the complexity of our own small things and by doing the small things, we create a magnet for the bigger things. It opens up a pathway, unblocks us, and sets us free to discover our limitlessness, our confidence, our happiness. This in turn frees our children.

Do the small things, one by one, day by day, moment by moment. Those *small things* clean up your energy, raising it in order to attract the energy of the *bigger things*.

Timed

When I was in college, and our apartment got very messy, my four roommates and I would occasionally call a "mad minute." We would set a timer and blast some music, then run around putting things away. Being five girls who felt we had better things to do than keep our apartment clean, this was an effective and painless way to make it presentable. With a timer set, we knew the cleaning-up session had a definite ending, and therefore we were all willing to jump right into the task.

Decades later, I've rediscovered the power of a simple timer. As we all know, *starting* something is often the hardest part. It takes our brains anywhere from five to twenty minutes to be fully immersed in a task. Up until then, it's a bit of a struggle; we're resisting, our minds are elsewhere, and if feels a bit like slogging through mud— thick, heavy, and not very enjoyable.

Several minutes into the task, though, we are fully engaged, in the flow, and unaware of time passing.

I bought myself a timer that I keep on my writing desk. When I am resistant to sitting down to write, or more often these days, to edit, I use the timer. I just have to do it until the sand runs through. When time is up, I'm free to go.

What usually happens is that once the time is up, I am fully into the process and don't want to stop right then.

But I *could* stop, because time is up. Knowing this is what gets me started.

The timer can be used for almost any task: cleaning up, going through paperwork, writing, studying, or exercising. I've even seen timers for kids' teeth brushing. They are two-minute timers shaped like little teeth with smiley faces. Clever!

There are a multitude of timers that range in cost from five dollars to fifty dollars. They come in all colors, and there are vintage styles, cherry finish, hand-blown glass, crystal, and antique-looking metal timers. You can find a timer from one minute to an hour. I chose a thirty-minute one.

It is fun to pick one out that serves your style and needs. Or maybe it's just me. I have a thing for timers. What else takes up such little space, looks appealing, and can pack such a punch in the time-management area of life?

Whatever it is you don't feel like doing, *just do it*.

Better yet, *time it*.

The Art of Self-Care

It has occurred to me that not everyone is as passionate about simplifying their lives as I am. Not everyone thinks that organizing a closet or an office is *fun*. Therefore, someone can like the idea of simplifying but never actually do it. Which is perfectly fine if the *idea* of it is only mildly appealing anyhow.

Like so many things—exercising, losing weight, getting healthy, changing careers, starting a beloved project, giving up sugar—it is easy to *like the idea of it* and quite a bit harder to *do it*. I suspect that to make any lasting change, we first need to *fall in love* with the idea of it.

We all know that doing something new, even if it's for the best, requires bypassing that well-worn groove our old habits have created in our brains. This new path can be steep and muddy, or thick and tangled with overgrown brush, making the first hundred or so steps difficult, prickly, and tiring. It requires so much energy and willpower just to keep going.

If the reason for starting down this path is not compelling enough, then who in their right mind would bother? It's too much damn effort, and life can be challenging enough without forcing ourselves to do unpleasant and daunting things on a regular basis.

If the reason for starting is not compelling enough. ...

Keep that in mind.

The goal *has to be compelling*. We have to be able to envision what we want and feel excited about the possibility. What would it look like? What would it feel like? Whatever our desire or goal is, big or small, we have to believe it will feel fantastic when we reach it.

We are creatures of habit, and if we cannot imagine the rewards of something different, then that well-trodden path—the one of least resistance—will pull us back every time. Why wouldn't it? It's familiar, easy, and takes very little effort to travel that way. These *samskaras*, as they are called in yoga, are deeply embedded patterns that don't change easily.

•

I like to think of self-care as an art. This implies that we are the artists of our own lives with the liberty to choose our medium. Maybe simplifying one aspect of your life does not appeal to you, but another aspect does. One artist may work with paints while another uses clay or metal or found objects, but they are all creating art. No one approach or medium is right for everyone. Just know that you are creating something beautiful, even though it may only be in one part of your life.

(I would argue that simplifying everything will help you reach any goal, whatever that is, but I don't want to be too pushy here. You can't do it all at once, so simplify the things that call to you.)

I use the term *self-care* because anything we really want that doesn't harm ourselves or others is, by its very nature, self-care. Greater fulfillment, satisfying relationships, more energy, resources, a sense of peace, a fit body, an aesthetically pleasing environment, getting more sleep, earning more money, or having more time for [fill in the blank] *is all self-care*.

So here comes my pep talk for making your desired result more compelling: Self-care feels amazing. It *is* worth it. The rewards *are* great.

What are they? Feeling lighter, freer, healthier, clearer, acquiring heightened intuition, increased energy, finding the right opportunities, meeting the right people, and discovering that great ideas just show up. You will be more in control of your life and you will meet all your needs.

Oh, and the momentum! One step down that new path leads to another and then another until it starts getting easier and you almost feel like you're running—and that's when the good things get easier, too. For example, have you ever noticed that when you work out, you want to eat healthy afterward? Or if you get rid of clutter in one room, you want to go on to the next? When you get enough sleep, you are clear-headed and efficient and everything goes more smoothly? One positive choice leads to the next, moving you forward. You gain traction, you notice little miracles, and you put your life in order.

Momentum is *awesome*.

Instead of trying to figure out ways to get rid of patterns you don't want in your life, you simply replace them or squeeze them out with the new things you *do want*.

Full disclosure: Left to my own devices or my natural temperament, I am *the worst* at breaking old habits and creating new ones. I have an Inner Brat who wants what she wants when she wants it.

I often want *absolute convincing* that a new pathway will be greatly rewarding before I begin something new. I need research and experience and possibly signs from a divine source that *this new way will be amazing*. The problem with this is that rewards often don't become apparent until we've begun. We can't experience it until we experience it.

I needed to know that writing, exercising, meditation, yoga, and mindfully choosing what I eat nearly every day—*even when I don't feel like it*—will be worth the effort.

But I couldn't know any of that for sure until I *did it*.

And neither can you.

You have to do it to feel the benefits. I can tell you that from firsthand experience, because now when I don't practice good habits, my day feels lacking. I am out of sorts; I am dissatisfied.

So, if you have some desire for something new and better, whatever that is, I want to save you weeks, if not years, of resistance. I want to tell you that if what you want comes from your Better Self, your Higher Self, your Real Self, *it will be so worth it!* It can't *not* be. I want to tell you that the burdensome path you are avoiding is littered with gold. You just won't see it until you're on it. Often, we want our mindset to change before we take action, but it's taking action that will change our mindset.

Self-care in every form will never let you down. Positive change is exciting and rewarding *every single time*, even when it starts out scary or daunting or difficult—perhaps *especially* when it starts out that way.

The act—*the actual physical act*—of heading down some difficult new path is pretty quickly rewarded. You'll notice early rewards within a few steps and won't have to wait much longer to notice fabulous results. And as you continue, step by step, the whole landscape comes into view and your own sweet masterpiece reveals itself.

A Discipline Alternative

I don't simplify because I am disciplined. I am disciplined because I simplified. Without simplifying, I don't stand a chance. I know that if I have too many things in my way—that is, on my agenda, in my head, or on my plate—I will never make it to that yoga class. I won't sit down and write if I am distracted by all the things I have to do afterward. If I am tripping over things on the way to my desk, both metaphorically and literally, I will never make it into the chair.

Eliminating all that I can, except what matters most to me, is how I stay consistent with those very things that matter most. Like most people, when I'm overwhelmed or tired, I am at my weakest. My method of finding order and consistency of purpose is to remove the things that keep me from what I want most. If I am clogged and cluttered with the extraneous, I can't see the path I want to be on, let alone move forward on it.

I simplify my diet by organizing my pantry and fridge. I streamline my wardrobe by keeping only what I like. I unriddle my exercise routine by committing ahead of time to a workout or a walk with my husband. I focus on what I want by eliminating everything from my agenda that I don't want or need, at least that is in my control. And only then, when I have pared down as much as I am able to, do I make the choices that give my life forward momentum. One good choice leads to the next, and good things happen.

If you want to make a change—any positive change—think of *subtracting* something before *adding* to your life. What can you let go of? Make some room for your spirit to breathe. That early discipline will simplify your life, and in turn give you greater discipline.

Digital Dichotomy

Oh, technology, I love you, but I resent you. You are useful, but I am sulking. You are invisible, but I trip over you. You are everywhere but nowhere. I need to have some command over you, but you get away. The files and folders and flash-drives. The downloads, documents, and drafts. A part of my world is housed up in screens and I am a tentative guest. How do I clear through the cobwebs of this computer clutter when I am unsure of what might crawl out?

I've got a handle on simplifying most areas of my life. Then there's technology. Here's my dirty little secret: My *everything digital* is nearly in chaos. Alas, I can no longer avoid it. My digital clutter is taunting me. Like a hoarder who doesn't know where to begin, or rather, doesn't *want to* begin, I think I have issues with technology. I notice the disarray. I feel the immensity. But. I. Just. Don't. Want. To. Face. It.

I don't mind organizing anything else. I welcome it, in fact. Bookshelves, paper files, lists, wardrobes, closets, kitchen cabinets, pantries, the fridge. Even the immense photo boxes made it to the top of my Sort Through List this year. I will gladly arrange, categorize, systematize, and coordinate. The progress is immediate and visible. I love being able to see everything in a drawer and know it's not overflowing with excess. I will gladly dispose of, wipe down, rearrange. But I can touch and maneuver those things with my hands.

Digital Housekeeping

Technology is digital. It's out there in the ether. In cyberspace somewhere. And that's harder to wrap my hands—and my head—around. It somehow zaps my motivation. My drive, if you will.

It's all so inordinate, so overwhelming. But we must tackle that which scares us once and for all, right? Unfiled documents that belong in specific computer folders, disorganized digital photos, out-of-date equipment that could be recycled. I will own my technology; my technology will not own me. Digital housekeeping—it's the thing I've avoided until now. I know it will make things easier and more pleasant in the long run. I just have to take that first step on the run. But I will have order. I will breathe through the process, and in the end, technology and I will become better friends. We will.

Digital Distractions

I am not sure at what point digital distraction becomes an addiction, but it's a slippery slope. Our children watch our actions, meaning that before we help them detox or manage their digital distractions, we must manage our own.

In his book, *Deep Work: Rules for Focused Success in a Distracted World*, Cal Newport says, "What we choose to focus on and what we choose to ignore plays a part in defining the quality of our life." We have to take a good, hard look at where we are putting our attention and then course-correct if need be.

Technology has kidnapped today's children. I once heard of a child saying, after too much time playing video games, "I feel so full but so empty." I thought it was good that this child had enough self-awareness to express the feeling of doing so much of something that it hijacks our brains and ultimately leaves us empty. I wish all children and teens and even adults could tune in to this sensation and compare it to how they feel after engaging in something wholesome and rewarding, like hiking, reading, having a good conversation, or doing fulfilling work. I hate for children to grow up feeling empty. The solution starts when we adults stop filling in the pauses of our own lives with distractions.

We need the pauses. Embrace them in this digital world so that we and our children can feel human again.

Bare Bones

I once had a 1,600-word essay I wanted to turn into a 1,000-word essay in order for it to fit into a specific publication. Cutting more than a third (thirty-eight percent to be exact) of a piece of writing may sound daunting, but I loved the challenge. It took me a fair amount of time and effort for sure, but it was well worth it. Every word had to count. I don't always do this in my writing, so it was good practice. I cut large chunks out of the essay, parts that I originally thought were essential, even priceless. I cut out words, then whole paragraphs, picking and choosing what could be sacrificed. Deciding what was essential and what was just fluff. In other words, I had to get down to the bare bones, and this required deciding: What are the bare bones? What *is* essential?

And this is what I love about simplifying. It's a creative privilege, a designing of one's own life in which you decide what to keep and what to get rid of. It's something I have not mastered, and will never truly master. Ah, but striving toward that lofty goal—no matter how many times I fall short—makes me happy. To keep only what we use or love; to buy only what we need; to only think only about what serves us well; to eat only what is good for us. To *say only what we mean.* What simply amazing results this could have!

The wonderful, demanding, awesome part of finding our bare bones is that our children are watching us. Our every action is being downloaded into their young brains as they prepare to copy us. Our words are being encoded in their developing brains. Our very energy is being absorbed into their consciousness. As if adulting weren't hard enough before we had children, now the stakes are higher. Habits, addictions, distractions, what we keep and what we shed, is all being noticed by them as if they are learning what it means to be human. They *are* learning what it means to be human. But the good news is, what is good for your children is good for you, too. Getting our act together for our children is not a burden but a blessing.

When I finished the essay, although there were parts missing or things left unsaid, I realized that I actually liked it better than before. What I had originally thought was essential wasn't. It was shorter, more concise, and somehow more powerful. The core of the message came through uncluttered.

Living is art, and we are the artists, the excavators, the sculptors. When the essential gets buried in too many details, we have to go digging to find it. We have to *find us*. And when we strive to keep the core of who we are front and center, dusted off and cared for, unencumbered by the extraneous, we feel whole and authentic—and this authenticity colors our parenting.

Our Nutritional Guru

*The mind's first step to self-awareness
must be through the body.*

—George Sheehan

While at a writing seminar, one woman wrote about how she used to get in fights with another girl every day after lunch before she knew it was caused by her body's severe mental and physical reaction to sugar and wheat. *Are you kidding me?* I thought. I actually asked her to repeat herself. I wasn't sure I heard her correctly. These foods took over her mind and body, as she described it. She reacted with rage, pummeling the other girl to the ground, causing her opponent to call her "crazy eyes."

As extreme as this sounded, it was a reminder of what I already knew. *What we eat affects the way we feel, and this truly is a gift.* When the information of what is good for us and what is not is overwhelming, all we have to do is tune in to our bodies. I am sure you are familiar with the mantra *listen to your body.* It's our key to knowing when we are pushing too hard or not hard enough. Even more importantly, it's where we feel our intuition—hence the terms "gut feeling" and "heart-wrenching." Our body is our instrument for *feeling everything.*

So, when it comes to diet, it really can be that simple. Listen to your body. It never lies. Though some of us have food allergies, all of us have foods that fuel us or make us sluggish, cranky, or bloated. Sugar makes me tired, as does anything made from flour: bread, pasta, baked goods, etc. I don't get the surge in energy I hear others talk about. I go right to the crash. A bowl of spaghetti leaves me wanting a nap. Bring on fruits and vegetables, particularly when raw. Water is my magic elixir. I feel icky when I eat anything packaged. I am slowly leaning into a vegan diet because I can no longer ignore what I know is good for me.

Though people react differently to different foods, it is generally accepted that hydrogenated oils, surplus sugar, or basically any processed food versus whole foods should not be consumed in excess. Some prefer to eliminate them altogether, challenging the cliché, "everything in moderation."

Foods should be healing and energizing. We should feel vibrant after eating them, not rundown. Live foods make us feel alive, and a higher vibration attracts higher-level experiences. You really can change your life by changing what you eat.

The information is out there. It isn't even that hard to find. Whatever we want to research—raw food diets, sugar addiction, gluten intolerance, foods that cause obesity. and foods that help us maintain a healthy weight—can be found in books and across the internet. There is certainly no shortage of good information. Want to know about the detriment of dairy? It's there. The merits of a vegetarian or vegan diet? That's there, too. The effects of alcohol on the brain? It's all there. But where do we turn when all this information is just too much? Inward. The body's wisdom is always available, silently telling us what to do. We just have to pay attention. That's the best information you'll find anywhere.

Mother of a Certain Age

I dictated these words to my fiftyish-year-old self who now has a habit of waking at three o'clock in the morning, thanks to changing hormones. This whole essay was in my head by the time I got up, giving up on sleep, two hours later. At least I was productive in my sleeplessness.

Why the insomnia? Perimenopause, I am told.

Sorry for the TMI, but this essay is about the body, the woman's body in particular, and even more precisely, *my* body, because I can't speak to *every* woman's body, of course.

I am going to cut right to the chase here. I have a theory that menopausal symptoms could be our bodies' way of urging us to finally *pay very careful attention to how we are treating them*. I am not saying that changes in women's bodies don't have biological and medical explanations. I get that they do. I *know* they do. I am saying that perhaps the antidote to the unpleasant changes that many women experience —weight gain, hot flashes, lethargy, insomnia, loss of libido—may be to get a little obsessive with self-care.

A couple of years ago I started having "spells." Seemingly out of the blue, I would feel faint, my heart would race, or else it felt like it was stopping for a second and I would come close to passing out. I didn't know what to call this because I had no idea what the cause was. A heart condition? A caffeine sensitivity? Anxiety?

I saw my doctor and he ordered an EKG and then a heart monitor and had me write down every time I felt my heart falling out of beat. When he determined that indeed I noticed each little flip that my heart had done, he said, "You are very in tune to your body." There was nothing to worry about, he thought. Just some common, harmless arrhythmia that many people don't even notice. So, my *abnormalities* were *normal* is what I was told.

The scary thing, though, was that the near-fainting spells would sometimes happen while driving. The summer before my youngest daughter began medical school, I had a spell while driving us home from an outing. I pulled over and my daughter calmly waited it out, talking to me until I was ready to switch places so she could drive us home. I guess I gave her a crash course in hypochondria. Or was it a panic attack?

I've been having menopausal symptoms *while still getting my period like clockwork every month*. How can I be fertile *and* menopausal?

Oh yeah, perimenopause—that period (no pun intended) that can last for years before menopause, when estrogen levels begin to fluctuate; it's as if the ovaries can't decide whether to produce or not, those fickle little ladies.

Another day I nearly passed out while inside a women's clothing outlet. I was in line to pay when a sales associate asked me if I was okay, because I had suddenly turned pale. She got me water and a piece of candy while I sat on a bench. She told me that this happens all the time, women dropping like flies in there, when it's too warm or too crowded. *Really? There are that many of us?* What a cliché I am!

I figured that what I had going for me in this whole set-of-new-symptoms time of life was what the doctor had confirmed: that I was very *in tune with my body*. This was the intuitive tool that would help me figure out what I had to accept and what I could change. I started to really pay attention to what I was thinking, eating, drinking, feeling, or doing when these symptoms emerged. I tuned in more than ever.

We live in a cerebral society, overthinking and rather obsessed with the mind. In the meantime, so much that we need to tune into, such as our memories, feelings, desires, and intuition, are stored *in the body*. The body tells us things before the mind has even caught on. It is the vessel for our nervous system, our creativity, and our energy. Taking care of our *whole* selves is critical to our wellbeing and ultimately our happiness.

Quality of life is directly related to the quality of the care we give ourselves. I think that "women of a certain age" are being urged to honor this. Don't hate me for saying this, but our symptoms are gifts. They're here to tell us to do better, to find a way to bring our self-care to a new level. For some, minor changes are all we need. For others, more drastic changes are required. But what is life if we are not changing?

Simply Yoga

Yoga is my answer to everything. Can't sleep? Practice yoga. Achy joints, back, knees? Yoga. Anxious, depressed, fearful, angry, sad, hyper? Yoga. Overweight, overwhelmed, overworked? Yoga, yoga, yoga. After practicing yoga for several years, I became certified to teach. To stop myself from sounding like an evangelist preaching yoga from the rooftops, I figured I'd lead some classes and therefore help make it available to those who came to it of their own free will. I am mostly a student, though, coming to my mat over and over because it brings me peace and presence in a distracting world. It offers me creative inspiration and some physical fitness.

What else besides yoga can so effectively improve physical and mental health, helping you make thoughtful decisions, put you in a good mood, and provide a deep inner peace? *And* it's legal! (Well, meditation can do all these things, too, minus the physical part).

Yoga is really meditation in motion. It's an exercise practice that gets you out of your head and into your body. It invites your own life-force energy to flow through you, healing and rejuvenating, strengthening and calming.

I've seen people fall asleep in yoga class, and I've seen someone break down and cry. That's because they needed to sleep and cry. Yoga brings about whatever needs to be. My favorite class I ever taught was for overweight students. They were all so serene by the end of class, their natural beauty shining through. I could almost feel the incremental change a single class brought about. I bet they instinctively knew that if they had the courage to commit to the program, the balance yoga brings about would give them a real chance at a healthier weight.

Since physical yoga has boomed in the West, some would say we've lost the depth of its origins. We've added music, as well as advertisements that boast how it will tone and strengthen and shape. We offer yoga in gyms, machines clanking outside the classroom door.

We have expensive classes and expensive clothes.

The physical part of yoga will produce benefits that only physical exercise can give, but that is only one aspect of yoga. Yoga goes much deeper than healing our ailments or building our strength and flexibility.

Patanjali's eight-fold path describes the whole of yoga: the guidelines for a meaningful and purposeful life. Patanjali was a sage from the Eastern world who recognized our cerebral limitations.

Patanjali's Eight Limbs of Yoga:

1. **YAMA** This first limb refers to the disciplines of nonviolence, truthfulness, on-stealing, right use of energy and nongreed.

2. **NIYAMA** The duties directed toward ourselves are the basis for this limb. These duties are cleanliness, contentment, discipline, self-study, and surrender to a higher power.

3. **ASANA** This refers to the postures, or physical aspect of yoga.

4. **PRANAYAMA** *Prana* refers to life-source energy. *Pranayama* are the breathing techniques of yoga that have the power to change our state of being.

5. **PRATYAHARA** The fifth limb refers to sense withdrawal. When sitting in meditation, we want to draw inward.

6. **DHARANA** Closely linked to the previous two, the sixth limb means a deep concentration, such as candle gazing, visualization, and focusing on the breath.

7. **DHYANA** The seventh limb is meditative absorption. This is when we become deeply and completely absorbed in our meditation, and everything else falls away.

8. **SAMADHI** The final limb of yoga is enlightenment, or bliss.

These eight limbs, or Yoga Sutras as they are also called, offer guidance on living a purposeful, mindful life. With study and practice, following the eight-fold path can lead a student of yoga to eventual liberation. But one of the many wonders of yoga is that you don't have to study these guidelines to benefit. You don't need to be an expert on the origins or purpose of yoga to reap the rewards. Higher consciousness or a spiritual path needn't be your goals, though they could, over time, become accidental byproducts of your practice. You can come to yoga because you want stronger biceps or to be more flexible. You can come to yoga because you don't have anything better to do on a Thursday evening. Even then, you won't escape its magic. You merely have to show up and breathe. It's that simple.

Sensitivity

My oldest daughter, the mother of twin toddlers, was recently ruminating over her inability to consume anything but the cleanest substances without suffering some pretty significant consequences. Any caffeine, even if consumed first thing in the morning, kept her from sleeping that night. A single alcoholic drink in the evening has the same effect. Gluten, sugar, dairy, and meat have a noticeable effect on her energy levels and mood. She is intolerant of many medications. The list of sensitivities could—and do—go on.

"You are the luckiest," I've said to her more than once. Essentially, you are forced to have a clean diet and live a healthy lifestyle. You cannot skimp on your self-care without real suffering. So, you have the opportunity to be the pinnacle of health and well-being!

Admittedly, I am putting a positive spin on some inconvenient sensitivities. I do sympathize with her, *particularly* on the caffeine front. I cannot imagine having gone through the toddler stage without my morning coffee.

I also know what it is like to be sensitive to substances. A too-tall glass of wine or an extra pour of coffee can send my heart racing these days. Consuming sugar or white-flour products make me want to take a nap. But I am not as sensitive to such substances, or to the loss of sleep they may cause, as my daughter is.

Recently, I finished reading a memoir called *We Are the Luckiest: The Surprising Magic of a Sober Life*. It is written by Laura McKowen, a woman who struggles with alcohol dependency. I immediately fell in love with her title and delved into the book, interested to learn about all the ways she thrived when she gave up her vice. And she is indeed thriving, but holy highballs, she takes the reader through some devastating stuff before reaching the *lucky* part.

Still, in the end, she is lucky and makes some immensely valid points about the rest of us being too okay or functional to ever contemplate giving up our diversions, whatever they may be. Are we thriving or just chugging along? Challenging our own impulses will never fill us with regret. But leaving them unchallenged could leave us depleted and unfulfilled.

So, for all you sensitive types or fed-up moms who cannot tolerate whatever it is you cannot tolerate—noise or stress or alcohol or sugar or negativity or *whatever* your poison is—chances are it's something that isn't really great for *anyone*. But you, the canary in a coal mine, your rock-bottom tolerance is always *right there* forcing you to course-correct with your next breath or the beating of your wild, tender heart.

You are the luckiest.

Soft Addictions

Soft addictions are seductive because they are easy and accessible ways to distract us from our feelings or the responsibility of living a bigger and better life. Soft addictions are sanctioned, even encouraged by society. We can become hooked on any activity or substance that has become a habitual distraction: television, shopping, social media, and sugar, just to name a few.

These are called *soft* addictions because they are seemingly harmless. And they *are* harmless, in moderation. But if not mindful, we can waste our entire lives engaging in so-called harmless habits. They may not land us in rehab or the morgue, but they will kill us softly, robbing us of time, energy, joy, growth, and achievements.

No one else will save us from our soft addictions. We can continue them for life, without so much as a sideways glance from others. But do we want to clutter up our lives with habits and distractions that weigh us down, hold us back, or model bad examples for the next generation?

Soft addictions satisfy a surface want but ignore a deeper need. The antidote to this, for parents and children, is to become aware of the deeper need. Admittedly, this is not easy because we have to come to this awareness by halting the very habit that is soothing us. This can be painful; as soon as we resist the distraction, we feel the discomfort. But if we make the conscious decision to get rid of a soft addiction, we cannot skip this step.

Moms typically have a lot on their plates, and I am not suggesting that you give up every frivolous pleasure in life. Pleasure is a worthwhile pursuit, after all. What I am suggesting is that if a pleasure seems to be excessive in its practice, become mindful of what is driving you. Are you enhancing your life or escaping from it? Often it is spiritual nourishment that we are truly in need of. We must nurture ourselves in a healthy way: take a walk, journal, talk to someone, or sit with the feelings that come up and breathe through them, knowing they won't last forever. We cannot declutter what we don't even know is there.

It is up to parents to notice when our children are heading down an addictive path, and to try to help them course-correct. One way to do this is to ask them if what they are reaching for is *really* what they need. Could they possibly feel lonely, anxious, bored? How can we help them address those feelings while discouraging them from simply numbing out? Habits formed in youth make all the difference, for better or worse.

The hedonistic theory is the idea that we are motivated by the pursuit of pleasure and the avoidance of pain. If that is true, why fight what is natural human behavior? There is nothing inherently wrong with trying to live a pleasurable life. I think that the key to stopping our pleasures from becoming dependencies is to ask the right questions: What *truly* nurtures you? What nurtures your child? Seek that.

Suggested Reading

The Alcohol Experiment
by Annie Grace (2018, Avery)

Atomic Habits
by James Clear (2018, Avery)

The Gentle Eating Book
by Sarah Ockwell-Smith (2018, Hachette Book Group)

The Happiness Project
by Gretchen Rubin (2018, Harper)

How Not to Die
by Michael Greger, M.D. (2019, Flatiron Books)

The Oh She Glows Cookbook
by Angela Liddon (2014, Avery)

The Power of Now
by Eckhart Tolle (2004, New World Library)

The Slight Edge
by Jeff Olson (2013, Greenleaf Book Group Press)

The Soft Addiction Solution
by Judith Wright (2006, Penguin Group)

Inspiration
& Intuition

The worst loneliness
is not being comfortable with yourself.

—Mark Twain

Cre-a-tiv-i-ty

The topic of creativity fascinates me. It is majestic and universal; everyone has an inner creative genius. That we have access to this could be our greatest gift. In one of my favorite books on creativity, *The War of Art*, author Steven Pressfield describes the perils of resistance to this gift.

Basically, resistance—otherwise known as *writer's block, self-sabotage, distraction, procrastination,* or in some cases, *addiction*—is everything we do to block access to our creative gifts or goals. Whenever we intend to embark on something innovative or artistic, or even simply attempt to create a new and healthy habit, resistance rears its ugly head. The author goes so far as to say that yielding to resistance *deforms the spirit.*

Ouch.

This makes me regret how much space I have allowed Resistance—with a capital R—to occupy in my life. I recognize myself in Pressfield's pages. I've yielded to resistance too many times to count.

Confronting Resistance

On a good writing day, I have that feeling of *I get to write!* I disappear into that divinely creative abyss, my words uncensored and untamed (there's time for editing later!). I'm enjoying the process even when it's difficult, but in those moments when the words come easily—or even when they don't, but the struggle produces the right word or sentence or page—the journey is sweet. At the end of those days comes the fulfillment of *having written.*

But when Resistance visits, it can stop me in my tracks. A distraction, an indulgence, a shiny new project, or simply Fear—with a capital F— sitting beside me, casting an impenetrable shadow on my motivation. Is it dramatic to say it deforms the spirit? If we are talking a day or a week of Resistance, then yes, perhaps that's dramatic. But over the course of a month or a decade or a lifetime, if we aren't careful, Resistance can derail us right out of our own best plans. If that doesn't warp the spirit, what does?

Overcoming Resistance

We all know that doing something new, or finishing what we've started, even if it's for the best, requires bypassing that well-worn groove old habits create in our brain. But the next day requires moving through Resistance yet again; diving into the stillness and poking around, to move forward. To do this you must push through the blocks and ignore the distractions. You must make friends with fear and allow it to accompany you on your journey. When it is in front of you, it will block your path, but when it is beside you, it will motivate you and push you onward. Here are the check points to keep you focused.

Breaking through the Resistance Checklist

✓ A Path Chosen and Followed

✓ Routine Builds Momentum

✓ Returning Day After Day

✓ Victory Over Resistance,
   a Spirit Soars!

Outside the Box

Many years ago, for three years, I lived in Texas with my husband. Texas seemed to own the sky and would sometimes open up into a display of light and sound that left us shaking. While driving anywhere, we could somehow see both our destination *and* forever, the endless road, a straight shot to eternity.

Both of us, having been born and raised in the Northeast, were homesick for our homeland and its magnificent hills and trees. I longed for New England to contain me again. To give me just the vision in front of me and the sense that I was *here* but not *there*. I missed the twisting and turning roads and knowing what was around the next corner only because it was *familiar*, not because I could actually *see* it. It felt more segmented and much less vast than Texas.

One season tiptoes into the next, haltingly, like mixing paint—some of this and some of that until the change is clear, the season defined. Still, we call them by separate names. They are winter and then spring. One and then the other. Words, like walls, organizing our year and our lives. It is a relief when one turns fully into the other; when it becomes *this* and not *that*.

This brings me to the popularity of the bento box, with its built-in compartments and my theory of why we love these. Originating as a Japanese lunch box, the bento box offers us a variety of foods carefully placed in a single portion, each item separated by the walls of the container. It looks so appealing and neat and special. No food touches the other. For some children, this is ideal.

How easy it is to compartmentalize with a bento box! In fact, you can't *not* compartmentalize with it.

Similarly, but much less tangibly, I came across a Life Box in a book recently. A diagram intended to help us balance our time and energy, it was divided into nine sections: *Family*, *Work*, *Contribution*, *Friends*, *Relationship*, *Leisure*, *Hobby*, *Personal Growth*, and *Alone Time*.

At first glance, the Life Box made sense, but then I thought of how many of my areas permeate other areas. My life is not nearly as segmented as that.

I'm guessing yours isn't either.

Sometimes, my leisure includes family, my alone time includes contribution or work, a hobby leads to personal growth, and so on. So much of life runs together that it really can't be separated, and I'm not sure I'd want it to be, though I suppose for some that would be simpler. It would certainly allow you to deal with just one area at a time and "shut out" other areas in order to focus on the one.

With a bento box, it's been done for you—all separate and tidy and clear and contained. It has boundaries. Clarity. You know what's there because you see it clearly in front of you. Every section has a clear boundary; nothing runs into anything else. It's just this thing, this material object of convenience. But metaphorically it's more. Much more.

It's how we imagine we might arrange our lives, or even just some days if we could. Yet deep down we know we wouldn't want to because we can't be contained. Not really. So, we appreciate the little things that give us the *feeling* of containment, or the illusion of it, if you will.

We want to contain time and label thoughts and people and this life. Simultaneously, I think, we want the openness of the sky and the prairie and all the vastness to hold that which we cannot contain—all that is eternal and timeless and has no limit.

Honor Thy Feelings

The goal of most parents is to raise children who will become happy, healthy, unaddicted, fully functioning adults. There are many things that go into raising a child, but one of the most essential is to honor *their* feelings.

If a child's emotional reality is not acknowledged or is deemed "unacceptable," the child will learn to repress her true self. When people become alienated from their true selves in childhood, they feel empty inside. This leads to the powerful and all-too-common effect of wanting to "fill oneself." There are plenty of distractions to fill up with, and sometimes, in the worst-case scenario, a distraction turns to a hardcore adult addiction.

In *Willpower's Not Enough*, Arnold Washton, Ph.D., writes, "The single most distinguishing trait of the addiction-generating family is that it fails to meet the dependency needs of its children … most often by failing to acknowledge the child's emotional reality."

Once again, what is good for your child is good for you. Have you addressed your childhood wounds? I recommend taking the ACE (Adverse Childhood Experiences) quiz in order to address any major adverse childhood experiences you may have buried long ago.

You will be much better at honoring your child's feelings if you acknowledge your own. Are you in touch with your feelings or do you turn to distractions to keep them repressed? Any one of us could—and too many of us do—spend our lives trying to avoid our emotional pain, whether past or present.

●

There are many cultural clichés designed to keep us from facing our wounds, and I am refuting all of them:

Time heals all wounds.

Wounds fester if not treated. There are many wounded adults walking around, which is why there are so many addictions. Therapy, education, love, and treatment heal wounds.

These things take time, but time alone does not heal wounds.

Leave the past in the past.

You can run from your past, but if your emotions were not honored, then the wound will follow you until your dying day unless you face it. You may think you left your past behind, but it will show up as impatience, soft or hard addictions, distractions, unhealthy relationships, guilt, perfectionism, underachievement, and even clutter. Denying our past keeps us stuck, affecting our energy on every level. Processing it sets us free.

What doesn't kill you makes you stronger.

Then how do we explain suicide, depression, and nervous breakdowns? Facing and healing your wounds makes you stronger; the wounds themselves do not.

God doesn't give you anything you can't handle.

It is my belief that people have free will, and hurt people hurt people. God does not make this happen, nor does he prevent it. So you may indeed experience more adversity than you can handle—particularly as a child—but it was not doled out by God. Rather it was doled out by people who have unhealed wounds.

Once you've lost contact with your authentic emotions, you lose contact with your body, since you have to detach from your body to no longer feel emotions coming through. This helps explain why so many women have body issues. Neglecting ourselves by over- or underexercising, over- or undereating, or overdrinking, for example, are ways to keep emotions dormant, stuffed underground.

•

So how do you honor your own and your child's feelings? With **Presence**. With being still, even if it is uncomfortable, and holding space for your own or your child's feelings. This doesn't mean you have to act on your feelings. Nor does your child. But to feel them, label them (disappointment, sadness, anger, frustration...), and let them pass through the body without judgment or interruption is the best gift you can give to yourself and your child.

Divine

As a preteen, I kept a journal that I addressed to my deceased grandfather. Not *Dear Diary* or *Dear God*, but *Dear Grandfather*. One day, in a moment of sibling torment, my sister grabbed the diary out of my hands and was confused by what she read. How could I explain? He was the only dead person I knew, and I thought he could be my connection to the divine. I believed that if I addressed my thoughts and feelings to someone beyond this earthly realm, I could somehow rise above my young-girl angst. And in some ways, I did.

Motherhood led me back to journaling, where I spilled everything onto the page: my thoughts, fears, and dreams. It kept me connected to my true self when motherhood could have easily swallowed me whole. I believed I was addressing God or my higher self. My belief that I could rise above my worries or my "lesser mind" grew stronger than ever.

Every single time I handed a problem over with my whole heart, I was shown the way forward. Every time I expressed an important desire or need, the best option became clear. And each time I expressed gratitude, my heart expanded and my blessings multiplied. My motherhood journal was my method of prayer. It was my method of asking questions both big and small. And keeping my life decluttered was my assurance that I'd be able to decipher the guidance. The absence of clutter, in all the forms addressed in this book, made it possible to tune in to higher realms.

I try to stay clear and uncluttered because I always want to hear that voice of intuition, of God and the divine guidance that is available. The answers come to me, whether I pray for myself or for others. There is no problem or dream too big for this knowing, and it is there for you, too. You just have to ask the questions and listen patiently for the answers.

Healing

Ever since I was a little girl, I knew I wanted to become a mother. I am happiest when I am nurturing and loving others. But being alienated from my own loving mother after my parents' divorce when I was four years old was a trauma that followed me into adulthood. Educating myself on pain and suffering led me to seek ways to rid it from my body, mind, and heart. When you are alienated from your primary caretaker, an alienation from the *self* occurs. In adulthood, I set out on a path to reconnect with my true identity, the self that was buried beneath my deepest wound. I guess you could say that the early and tragic separation from my mother led me to a deep desire to become *uncluttered* in order to find the path back to my essence. Yet, as much as I wanted to be healthy and cleansed, I had only a vague idea about how to do it. It was like knowing my destination without having a good roadmap.

But at least I had an idea where to start—where I was. I went to therapy and visited healers and asked God to bring my most painful memories to the surface so that I might purge myself of them. I connected with people who had similar stories. All of this was useful for a time, as was my own search for truth. And one cannot be whole while avoiding painful truths of the past.

Then there came a time, not so long ago, that I finally discovered—or rather uncovered—that the path to my best self was simple. The seemingly small choices I made every single day either brought me closer or further from my truth. Anything that needed to be brought to light and healed within me would be if I remained mindful and in the present. All I had to do was choose the next right thing.

If there is too much inner and outer extraneous matter, we will avoid—or never find—the way to healing. On the contrary, it is hard to be *uncluttered* and remain lost, because

the way forward is revealed in the open spaces.
Clarity will lead you home every time.

Allowing Fear

Most of my fears can be avoided—fear of roller
coasters, walking down dark alleyways alone
at night, death by alligators. I simply don't ride
roller coasters, walk through alleyways, or jump
in swamps.

But there's another kind of fear that serves
us well to embrace, or at least face, and that's
the fear that we feel when facing a hard truth
or a new challenge. It may be the fear of grief
or a difficult change or even the sparkling,
terrifying, exciting idea that awaits you when
all else falls away.

It's the fear at the bottom of the excess or the
end of the distractions. The one that's there when
you peel off, throw out, clean up, or clear away.

That fear that you work hard to keep at bay may even present itself as boredom or restlessness, but if allowed to surface, it could launch you forward into creativity or healing or success in a new endeavor.

You'll be serving your children well if they grow up witnessing you sitting with discomfort long enough to *go through it* rather than *bury it*. Rather than recoil, you become sure-footed. You are damn sure you aren't turning back, because to do so would feel like self-betrayal.

So, to sum up, feel the fear, whatever that is for you. Boredom? Restlessness? Memories? Breathe deeply. Invite it in. It won't stay long. Or maybe it will, but it definitely won't kill you. In fact, it may do the opposite. It may enliven and enthuse you and launch you forward into something new and wonderful. The *something new* doesn't necessarily mean a new project, career, or lifestyle. The new could mean healing, forgiveness, expansion, or simply peace. In essence, a new, rejuvenated you.

Take a moment.

What are you afraid of? Go there.

Dissonance

In my earliest memory of church, I am standing next to my grandmother, reciting a prayer by rote memory: "Lord I am not worthy to receive you..."

Why am I not worthy? my five-year-old self wondered. *What have I done?* The prayer was coming through my lips. My thoughts about it were coming from my head. My heart was sort of disconnected from the whole experience.

"...only say the word and I shall be healed."

All around me people were broken. I would come to believe that it takes more—so much more—to be healed than *only saying the word* in church. It takes things like courage, desire, truth, reflection, and yes, faith. My faith would come much later though, and have very little to do with a Catholic mass, or so it seemed. It would have much more to do with sitting with my confused self than with a congregation; more to do with *uncovering* worthiness than *denying* it.

•

When my three children were of the age to attend church, I did what every lapsed Catholic was doing back then. I dressed them up a bit and, with my husband, who somehow thought I was equipped to make this all-important choice, took them there. I felt like a bit of an impostor, because I just never really liked going to church. Besides, I'd taken up meditation and yoga, one hour of which gave me more peace in my heart than any church service ever had. I loved devoting time to strengthening my connection to the divine, and to my own soul, but for me it was a private endeavor.

You could say it's a personal preference. There are many paths to God, right? So how do you go about choosing for an entire family?

I honestly don't know, but there is no one right way and I think it has something to do with trusting yourself.

Anyhow, I dutifully signed our oldest up for the First Communion classes, because in the moving sidewalk that is Catholicism, when it's time, it's time. This meant that she had to attend a class before the church service each Sunday, and then also attend mass after the class. She was six years old. By the time mass rolled around, she was hungry and bored and feeling about as Christlike as a famished banshee.

And just to add to my cognitive dissonance, one of our daughters asked, "Why is the priest always a man?"

I think I said something profound like, "Um... no good reason?" That was as profound a response as I could muster on the fly. I thought she was a bit young to have a discussion on patriarchy or the history of Christianity or the merits and pitfalls of organized religion.

So that's how we spent our Sunday mornings for a short time, making everyone stop whatever activity they were engaged in to get ready for a round of church. Gather the snacks and the nursing baby and take the playing children *out of the moment where God resides* because it's the Lord's day and who needs peace anyway?

On one such Sunday morning, which is etched in my memory, my husband tried to gently and quietly carry our daughter out of church, as she had grown increasingly agitated. When they got halfway down the aisle, toward the exit, I heard my darling, free-spirited daughter's explosive cry:

"I HATE CHURCH!"

Sometimes parenting includes a lesson or two in humility with those embarrassing and awkward moments of silence.

And *now*...let us pray.

The Mystery of Ideas

For a moment, but preferably a lifetime, I am asking you to consider the possibility that ideas and inspirations may come from inexplicable sources, whether from something divine and alive, from your own soul, or as some may say, even from God Herself. An idea can come out of a desperate plea or, more often, from a simple opening created in stillness.

However you choose to think about the ideas that come to us or through us, there is this universal truth: *We all get them.*

We most definitely do not always notice them, or invite them, or act on them, but we get them. Much of the time we swat them away like flies. Why? I guess we are often too busy, too comfortable, too skeptical, too insecure, or just too darn attached to inertia. It's just easier to ignore a good idea than engage it.

But ideas cannot survive on their own. They need people—willing, creative humans—to objectify them. In her book, *Big Magic: Creative Living Beyond Fear*, Elizabeth Gilbert writes:

"Ideas are driven by a single impulse: to be made manifest. And the only way...is through collaboration with a human partner."

Ideas can be as varied as the people who host them. What I am talking about are the creative ideas that spur us to either make something new or change something old. An idea may come as a whisper, or it may include a bodily sensation such as excitement mixed with nervousness. And if you're truly lucky, the idea may grip you with such force that there is only one way to go with it: *forward*.

We are creative beings, after all, and I think we are just happier when we are creating *something*, even if just a clever and satisfying tweak to our environment or routine. But we are happiest when it is something big.

So how can we invite ideas, the kind from another realm, that bring joy and change and creations of all kinds?

Well, since you ask, here's my answer based on my experiences as well as from a boatload of reading on the topic (because it intrigues me to no end).

Eliminate Chaos.

Eliminate all of it, or as much as you can. Clear the decks, because ideas prefer a clear path. They cannot reach you if they are tripping over the clutter in and around you. Clean up the mess, literally and figuratively, and ideas will stand a chance of getting your attention.

Take Care of Yourself.

You know what to do. Eat well, sleep well, get exercise, and keep a reasonable schedule.

Pay Attention.

When you receive that idea, don't swat it away. It may hang around for a while, and you may get another chance at it, but eventually it will give up on you and move on. We're all going to miss out on some ideas, but don't let them all get away— particularly the big, scary ones because those are rare and amazing. The bigger the commitment, the bigger the payoff.

Follow Your Curiosities.

Every new invention, creation, positive change, or idea starts with a question. *What about this? What if I tried that? I wonder who, what, where. ..?* Consider that your curiosities are gifts leading you somewhere new. I don't care if you are ninety years old, we all have curiosities. Have the conversation, take the new road, ask the darn questions. Even when it is inconvenient or unsettling or out of your comfort zone, *don't accept what you know as all you want to know.* Allow curiosity. Follow it. Curiosity may have killed the cat, but satisfaction brought it back. It will do the same for you and the human spirit.

Take Your Ideas Seriously.

Please. I don't mean in a rigid, stoic sort of way. I mean consider them. Play with them. Don't be quick to dismiss them. Ideas come to us for a reason. Focus on an idea. Obsess over it if you have that luxury, but at least commune with an idea in a consistent manner as soon as you can. Devote yourself to an idea and watch it grow. Be afraid if you must, but do it anyway. Make mistakes, ask for help, feel silly trying, inconvenience someone, but follow that idea. It's yours.

It *chose* you.

The least you can do is respect it.

Capturing Inspiration

Long before I ever had a laptop, back in the day when I was tapping at keys on a typewriter, I kept various writing notes in a decorative box, the kind you find at a craft store for keeping photos or other treasures in. Raising young children limited my writing time, but just taking out that box and holding it got my creative juices flowing. I always knew I'd get back to my work-in-progress when I could steal time again.

My daughters have grown and moved out,

and like Virginia Woolf, I now have A Room of My Own in which to muse and write and pile up essays and book chapters on my laptop. But despite the space and all the technology available to me today, I have not outgrown The Box.

My box has changed in size and type only, having now upgraded to one I found at Staples that fits my four-by-six-inch index cards full of notes, quotes, and ideas. It comes with matching dividers and an adjustable follow block, keeping all cards upright and orderly. If one can fall in love with a box, I surely have.

I store essay and blog ideas, memorable quotes, notes from books I've read, and anything else that may inform my writing. For jotting down notes away from home, I simply carry a little green index card holder, one that easily fits into a purse or bookbag. Notes from this can be transferred into the box later.

Why not just store all these notes digitally? Because, having so many tangible "moving pieces" to work with moves me toward the finished product in a way that feels so satisfying to me. It's all part of the creative process.

My oldest daughter and a mother of two struggles to find time to create. I recently reminded her of her art journal; of the importance of getting her ideas down on paper so that they don't fade away like a poignant dream that can no longer be recalled. Whether in a box, a journal, or digitally, capturing our ideas in a way we can easily refer to later is half the fun and half the progress.

Placing holders of inspiration, nuggets of information, parts of the whole, bit by bit—even with small pockets of time—will bring any vision into focus.

Trust

As parents, we want what is best for our children. Sometimes we can get overzealous in trying to figure out what *best* is and we forget to trust their unfolding. Our eagerness to guide can become an impediment to their natural growth.

It is very natural for children to want to please their parents. This is to their advantage when we are teaching them valuable habits or keeping them safe from harm. But because we are in a position of authority and power, it is so important to be mindful of our influence. We want to think we know what is best for our children, but sometimes admitting that we do not always know is the greatest freedom that we can give them.

Labeling children, telling them what they should study in school, sharing our opinions too freely, can cause fragmentation. Children want to have our acceptance, but if their authentic expressions do not align with their parents' wishes, they may begin to repress their true selves.

Parenting is an enormous undertaking. But it is so much harder if we don't trust that our children have come into this world as whole and divine human beings. They need our love and nurturing and guidance. They also need us to *allow* them to become who they are.

Before you share your thoughts with them, ask them what *they* think. Give them control over their own lives as much as they are capable. Encourage them to follow their own inner guidance. In trusting them, they will trust themselves.

One of my most valuable takeaways from two decades of parenting is realizing it is better to talk less and listen more; ask opinions more often than giving them, and trust more than doubt.

We may know our own child well, and we have far more life experience, but we don't have *their* life experience, *their* precise desires and interests, and *their* soul's purpose. They are ours but not ours. They are on their own journey and we've been entrusted to help them *and* stay out of the way. *I am not God* and *I do not know* are humble phrases that will serve us, and them, well.

What's Next

One of the most exciting things about simplifying is what comes after. Simplifying clears the way and begs for an answer to this question:

What do I want?

After clearing your home or your mind or your schedule—and hopefully all three—there is this space that feels like a spectacular opening, an invitation. Sometimes what fills up that space is the understanding that *I already have everything I want and now I can enjoy that more*. This is a beautiful thing. But it is in our human nature to grow, so, even if we have most of what we want, there is often something else. I think our desires can be the touchstones for that growth.

Touchstones were once used for testing alloys of gold. *Is this real? Is this valuable?*

What is real and valuable to you?

We have to make room for that which is meaningful to us. We have to give up something of our lower nature in order to obtain something of our higher nature. Staying full of all kinds of clutter can be comfortable, like a cushion or a barrier between what we have now and what we don't dare ask for. We want to hush that thing we want that whispers to us because it's too big, too scary, too improbable, or, God forbid, others might not approve.

Maybe all we want is to be uncluttered. To be clear and free, mind, body, and soul. It is the simplest thing and the tallest order. The world pulls us every which way and we have to choose. We have to navigate the denseness of daily life.

Sometimes, rarely, we get what we want instantly. More often, there is much work to do to get us there, but at least we are on our way. Anything I've gotten that I wanted came after either writing down my desire (my form of prayer, in a way) or saying it aloud. The words *I WANT* hold power. They add clarity, focus, priority.

The thing is, when we know what we want, it becomes painfully clear when we choose something that is *not that*. We know when we've chosen in the direction that is *away from* our desires, and it feels all wrong, like heading east when we should be heading west. Our desires and goals—at least the reasonably healthy ones— are a reliable compass.

Becoming an Uncluttered Mother

When you've put forth the effort and mindfulness day after day to unclutter your environment, your mind, body, and soul, you will be rewarded beyond all measure. Clarity, joy, and peace will be just some of the gifts you receive. It is a journey back to yourself—the authentic, powerful you.

Uncovering the core of who you are and living from that place is an amazing gift to your children and the only way to truly live your best life. No matter your past, do one thing today that sets you on this path. Is there something that no longer serves you that you can release or give away? Someone you can forgive? If you are consistent, even in seemingly small ways, you will come to trust yourself about the ways to becoming an uncluttered mother.

Simple in actions and in thoughts,
you return to the source of being.

—Lao Tzu

Think progress, not perfection. But set your sights high, Mama. You deserve the best.

Suggested Reading

Big Magic: Creative Living Beyond Fear
by Elizabeth Gilbert (2016, Riverhead Books)

Childhood Disrupted: How Your Biography Becomes Your Biology, and How You Can Heal
by D. Jackson Nakazawa (2016, Atria Books)

Embrace Your Magnificence
by Fabienne Fredrickson (2014, Hay House)

The Seat of the Soul
by Gary Zukav (2014, Simon & Schuster)

Waking Up: A Guide to Spirituality Without Religion
by Sam Harris (2015, Simon & Schuster)

The War of Art
by Steven Pressfield (2012, Black Irish Entertainment LLC)

Afterword

It wasn't until my children were nearly grown
that I began to write about motherhood and all
the ways in which I had tried to keep the journey
mindful. I suppose that was the way it was
meant to be, giving me two decades of parenting
to reflect on the lessons I'd gleaned, thoughts I
could not always extract while in the thick of
raising three daughters. The words that I offer
in this book come from what I know now, which
is clearer than what I knew then. Like all of us,

I learned as I went along, and often fell far short of my ideals. My daughters are the wonderful human beings that they are today not just because of my mothering, but perhaps in spite of it as well.

Motherhood is a journey that continues, that will continue throughout my life. Like being a woman and a writer, it is not only a role I play but also a deeper part of who I am. Now I have two granddaughters, too, and am learning all over again how much the heart can expand.

I am honored that you have taken the time to read my words. It is my greatest hope in writing this book that something in it brings you lasting peace on your journey.

With love and gratitude, Dana

About the Author

Dana Laquidara is an award-winning writer whose work has appeared in *The Huffington Post, Mamalode, Literary Mama, Brain Child Magazine, Boston Mamas, The Grub Daily,* and *Spirituality & Health Magazine.* Her topics speak to the heart and include wellness, creativity, parenting, simplifying, and healing old wounds, all of which she finds to be interwoven. She has also participated in several Boston Moth storytelling events and took first place while performing a piece from her memoir-in-progress.

Dana's degrees are in Education and Holistic Health Studies. Prior to forging her path as a writer, she taught elementary school and then adult yoga. Still an avid yogi and a lifelong student of personal growth, Dana is the mother of three grown daughters, and lives in Massachusetts with her husband.